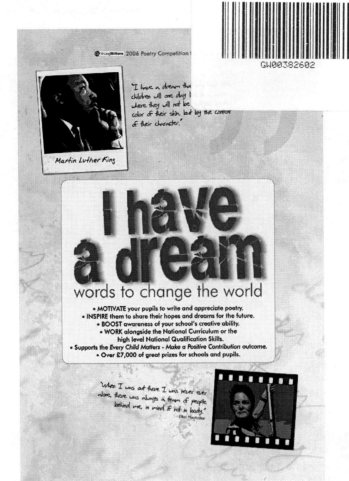

2006 Poetry Competition

"I have a dream that my four little children will one day live in a nation where they will not be judged by the color of their skin, but by the content of their character."

Martin Luther King

I have a dream
words to change the world

- MOTIVATE your pupils to write and appreciate poetry.
- INSPIRE them to share their hopes and dreams for the future.
- BOOST awareness of your school's creative ability.
- WORK alongside the National Curriculum or the high level National Qualification Skills.
- Supports the Every Child Matters - Make a Positive Contribution outcome.
- Over £7,000 of great prizes for schools and pupils.

"When I was out there I was never ever alone, there was always a team of people behind me, in mind if not in body."

- Ellen MacArthur

- Future Visions
Edited by Claire Tupholme

 Young**Writers**

First published in Great Britain in 2006 by:
Young Writers
Remus House
Coltsfoot Drive
Peterborough
PE2 9JX
Telephone: 01733 890066
Website: www.youngwriters.co.uk

SB ISBN 1 84602 662 8

Foreword

Imagine a teenager's brain; a fertile yet fragile expanse teeming with ideas, aspirations, questions and emotions. Imagine a classroom full of racing minds, scratching pens writing an endless stream of ideas and thoughts . . .

. . . Imagine your words in print reaching a wider audience. Imagine that maybe, just maybe, your words can make a difference. Strike a chord. Touch a life. Change the world. Imagine no more . . .

'I Have a Dream' is a series of poetry collections written by 11 to 18-year-olds from schools and colleges across the UK and overseas. Pupils were invited to send us their poems using the theme 'I Have a Dream'. Selected entries range from dreams they've experienced to childhood fantasies of stardom and wealth, through inspirational poems of their dreams for a better future and of people who have influenced and inspired their lives.

The series is a snapshot of who and what inspires, influences and enthuses young adults of today. It shows an insight into their hopes, dreams and aspirations of the future and displays how their dreams are an escape from the pressures of today's modern life. Young Writers are proud to present this anthology, which is truly inspired and sure to be an inspiration to all who read it.

Contents

Elmbrook Special School, Enniskillen

Foxhills Technology College, Scunthorpe

Hope High School, Salford

Wellington College, Belfast

The Poems

The Shoebox

This shoebox used to be mine
But it will help other people feel fine,
I feel for Romania's boys
Who have no other toys.

But this shoebox is worth a lot,
It might be all that he has got.
It could help a family
To live well and happily.

But yet people always struggle
Among the rubbish and the rubble;
With just a good shoebox appeal
We could help them really feel
As well and happy as you and me.

David Little (14)
Aughnacloy College, Aughnacloy

Shoebox

I wish I could see
How happy they'll be;
Young and old,
Frail and cold.

I wish I could see
How happy they'll be;
Mums with their boys
When they get their toys.

I wish I could see
How happy they'll be;
With the extra things we had,
Will make them so glad.

Heather Badger (14)
Aughnacloy College, Aughnacloy

Help The Little Children

Just sit down at your table
In your warm, warm house.
Think of all your lovely food,
And a fireplace full of wood.

While on the soil they're lying
On the cold, cold ground.
You, lying on your soft, soft bed;
While their parents are dying
On the hard, hard ground.

Then for a little while
Take a little minute;
Those old used things that we've had
Will make those people feel so glad.

Amy Robinson (14)
Aughnacloy College, Aughnacloy

Just Look

Just look around and see what you've got.
Things that you have, and others have not.
Please give to the poor in time of need,
Something that won't feed on your greed.

We've sent shoeboxes - one hundred and twenty,
To children with nothing while we have plenty.
In these we send for Christmas time,
Gifts to make their faces shine.

Jemma Hanthorne (14)
Aughnacloy College, Aughnacloy

Take One Moment And Think

Take one moment and think, my friend;
While we sleep in a comfortable bed,
Others sleep on a hard stone floor
Because many of them are so poor.

Some sleep while others weep,
Some steal to make ends meet,
Others even eat raw meat,
While others have cold feet.

Take one moment and think, my friend;
While we eat and escape from the heat
And sit on very cosy seats,
So we give shoeboxes to make
Christmas meet.

Matthew Crawford (14)
Aughnacloy College, Aughnacloy

Nothing Else Matters

They are so close, no matter how far,
Couldn't be much more from the heart,
But they need so much more,
And nothing else matters.

Lots die along the way,
This happens every day,
All these words I don't just say,
And nothing else matters.

Not knowing, anything new,
All those people feeling blue,
We'll do everything we can,
And nothing else matters.

They are so far away from us,
Nothing but bodies, covered in dust,
While we live a life of lust,
They know that nothing else matters.

Timothy Law (14)
Aughnacloy College, Aughnacloy

What Does It Take?

Christmas is a happy time
We have Diet Coke with lime

Lots of parties,

Lots of fun
But think of those who will have none

Thousands of children on the street
Searching and stealing to make ends meet
Rubble, rumble everywhere
What will it take to make us aware?

Children lying in dark alleys
With nothing in their little bellies
We look at the faces, young and old
As they open their shoeboxes, bright and bold.

Katie-Anne Read (14)
Aughnacloy College, Aughnacloy

Do They Know It's Christmas Time?

Christmas time; what a joy,
But not for some unlucky boy.
We see presents and Christmas trees,
All he sees is poverty.

We are lying in our beds,
When they are thinking in their heads
If there is a God above,
Why does He not show His love?

Our house is warm
And full of love,
But they are lucky
To have a glove.

And they say,
'People, people,
Can't you see,
What the world is like for me?

If you could only
Come and see,
What your shoebox
Will do for me.'

Nicola Jones (14)
Aughnacloy College, Aughnacloy

Take From The Rich And Give It To The Poor

Take from the rich,
And give it to the poor,
There'll be no more homelessness,
No more sleeping on the floor.

Chorus:
Take from the rich and give it to the poor;
Take from the rich and give it to the poor;
No one shall die a lonely soul,
If we take from the rich and give it to the poor.

Some people die at an early age,
While they could live to a ripe old age,
This is what happens when you live in the sewers,
So let's take from the rich and give it to the poor.

Chorus:
Take from the rich and give it to the poor;
Take from the rich and give it to the poor;
No one shall die a lonely soul,
If we take from the rich and give it to the poor.

Dale Givans (14)
Aughnacloy College, Aughnacloy

I Have A Dream

I have a dream that you can walk down
the street without being judged
on the way that you look,
Fat or thin, tall or small, black or white

I have a dream you'll dream too.

Rebekah Moffett (13)
Dunluce School, Bushmills

I Have A Dream

I have a dream that one day someone will end
Wars
And sectarianism
That everything will be peaceful.
We don't have to get on
But it's better than
People dying
Over it.
We would learn to be all counted
As *one!*

Melissa Bolt (13)
Dunluce School, Bushmills

I Have A Dream

I have a dream, a fantasy
To play for Liverpool and England too
To be an electrician, make life worth the while
Sleeping through the darkness, making girls love life
I believe in dreamers
Loving all the things I see and do
I believe in dreamers
When I see Gerrard in Liverpool
I'll cross the dam - I have a plan.

Owen Craig (13)
Dunluce School, Bushmills

If Only . . .

A world with no war,
more peace within.
Equality no matter what . . .
we all can win.

The world and I,
we are still strong
and will hold on,
till our battle's won.

A world with no war,
more peace within,
it is possible,
so let's begin . . .

Caroline Getty (13)
Dunluce School, Bushmills

I Have A Dream

I have a dream,
Not just for me,
But for the world,
And everyone in it.
That one day we
Will all be equal,
No sadness,
No loneliness,
But happiness everywhere.
To make my dream come true,
Not I or you,
Can do it,
So come on,
Get together and
Make my dream
Come true!

Amanda McMaster (13)
Dunluce School, Bushmills

I Have A Dream!

I have a dream,
To be a rainbow,
To sit high in the sky
And overlook everyone.
We could play games
Like hide-and-go-seek,
And I would hide behind the clouds,
While others would hide on the ground.
I have a dream,
To be a rainbow,
I would make everyone
Happy and bright,
So all the sad faces would go inside.
I would have a meaning
For every colour,
Red for love,
Orange for light,
Yellow for laughter,
Green for grass,
Blue for the sky,
Indigo for respect,
Violet for friendship.

If my dream ever came true,
There would be a pot of gold at the bottom.

Emma McQuilkin (13)
Dunluce School, Bushmills

I Have A Dream

I have a dream
That racism will end
That barriers will be broken
And friendships will be made
That white people will wave
To black people in the street
And the black people will wave back
That is my dream
What is your dream?

Christopher Archibald (12)
Dunluce School, Bushmills

Animal Cruelty

Here I sit in a box
In the middle of nowhere
Beside a field.
I used to have a home.
My owner has thrown me out
Into the cold.
We used to play
In the back garden
But now all I have is
My box, no food,
No bones,
No toys.

Jill Stirling (12)
Dunluce School, Bushmills

I Have A Dream

I have a dream
That the world will
Be full of peace

No more war
Or sectarianism

That we can all live
Together

To accept each other
The way we are.

Lois Carson (12)
Dunluce School, Bushmills

Oh Come Home

Every night I sit near the window
Dreaming he'll come home
I miss him every day
But that won't bring him home
Every minute I think *is he alive or dead*?
My dream is for him to come home
While I lie in my bed.

Andrew McCracken (12)
Dunluce School, Bushmills

I Have A Dream

I deal,

H appy and healthy people,
A Heaven on Earth,
V iolence gone,
E qual rights,

A proper home to live in,

D roughts at an end,
R ain in Africa,
E quality,
A lot of fun,
M y ideal world!

Jodie McFarlane (13)
Dunluce School, Bushmills

I Have A Dream

I have a dream.
A dream of passion.
I want to do something,
Anything good.
That my name shall be remembered.
When the dust of my bones
Is lying in a coffin in 1,000 years,
May everyone remember my name.

Simon Friel (13)
Dunluce School, Bushmills

I Have A Dream

I have a dream
A dream that, hopefully, will come true
No more hunger, that will do

I have a dream
A dream that hopefully will come true
To play for Man U
Even though I don't support them
But that will still do

Imagine the world like Heaven
Not like Salou

Heaven is the best place
A wish has come true.

Gavin Darragh (12)
Dunluce School, Bushmills

I Have A Dream Come True

I have a dream come true
That maybe one day I'll find you
You might say I'm a dreamer
Living in the world as one

I have a dream come true
That maybe I'll go to Salou
You can take the future even if you fail
There is something good in everything
I have a dream come true.

Pamela Glass (12)
Dunluce School, Bushmills

I Have A Dream

I hope that there is no more fighting,
That we have a world of peace,
No more deaths in the world,
No more fire and no more burglaries

I have a dream,
No more water shortages,
People get food,
No more wastage of food,
I hope people who are poor have heat,

I have a dream,
Rich people will give poor people money,
No killing, murders or suicides,
I wish the world would be safe and good.

Gavin Hickinson (12)
Dunluce School, Bushmills

I Have A Dream

I have a dream.
I wish I could
change the world.

I wish I could
help the kids
who die from poverty.

If only I could
help those kids
who get beaten
by their mums and dads.

Perhaps one day
my dream will come true.

Ewan Houston (14)
Dunluce School, Bushmills

I Have A Dream

I hate the war in Iraq
where all we do is attack.
Don't they know there is no need to fight
because Saddam has been captured?

I think they only fight in Iraq
because they need oil to help trains
on the tracks.
I wish they would just pull out -
he
has
been
captured.

Christopher Cunningham
Dunluce School, Bushmills

Worth It

I hope that I wrote
Something worth writing
I hope I said
Something worth saying
I hope I went
Somewhere worth going
I hope I dream
Something worth dreaming.

Chris Hanson (15)
Dunluce School, Bushmills

I Have A Dream

Why is there so much fighting?
Why do children starve?
If you can do something about it
Then try, try, try.

What's the difference between black and white?
We all have the same heart
So make peace
If you can do something about it
Then try, try, try.

What's up with animal cruelty?
Would you want to be hit every day
With sticks and fists?
If you can do something about it
Then
Try, try, try.

Cameron Grundle (14)
Dunluce School, Bushmills

I Have A Dream

I have a dream . . .
No animals being killed for their skin
No foxes being shot or run over by man

No bears, no lions being killed for their meat
No fish, no whales being stuck in nets and dying

I have a dream . . .
Pandas survive not being extinct
And living and breeding and living life to the fullest

I have a dream . . .
No pups being abandoned or drowned
But living with their owners until they die.

Glenn McAfee (14)
Dunluce School, Bushmills

I Have A Dream - The African Kids

They're poor, hungry,
starving African kids.
They're sad, need help,
Survival for the African kids.

No food, no water, no crops,
unhealthy bones for the African kids.
Their family is dead,
Homeless little African kids.

We give them our help,
lucky African kids.
More money, water and
survival for the African kids.

Gareth McAuley (13)
Dunluce School, Bushmills

I Have A Dream

Now and then I have a dream
The word *war* is what I dream
Is it bad? Is it good?
None of us will know
And I always think *will my dad or friend have to go?*
But unfortunately none of us will know.

David Matthews (13)
Dunluce School, Bushmills

I Have A Dream

D reams are funny. They capture your emotions.

R eality or fiction. It's still a dream.

E very dream has an ending. Even the stupid ones.

A long the seashore. Or maybe in a gutter. A dream's a dream.

M ermaids or monster, it doesn't matter. But when you have a
dream, it's magical.

S cary dreams make you jump. Dreams about fairies I don't like,
but girls do!

Andrew Platt (13)
Dunluce School, Bushmills

I Have A Dream

Every animal deserves a chance
They're not just a present for Christmas
They need love and affection
Just like everyone else
They don't deserve
To be trapped in cages
They need a home
Where they can feel safe and retreat to
Animals all over the world
They deserve a chance
They're not just a present for Christmas.

Lewis Hodges (13)
Dunluce School, Bushmills

I Have A Dream

I heard about these disasters that

H appened in the world
A fter Christmas the tsunami came
V ery much destruction
E veryone's houses were destroyed

A nother world disaster affecting the world

D reaming of a way I can help
R escue teams, their lives risking
E mergency rooms filling up
A nother disaster ends but not forgotten
M y dream ends.

Ryan McGowan (13)
Dunluce School, Bushmills

I Have A Dream

I have a dream that everyone would be friends
It would be fantastic and the friendship
Would never end

Then no one would get bullied or hurt
Instead they would love each other
And say things like, 'You big flirt'

If only things would be so good
Nothing is ever that simple but it should

I wish we could all work as a big team
That would be my perfect world
And, of course, my perfect dream.

Charlene O'Neill (13)
Dunluce School, Bushmills

I Have A Dream

I close my eyes,
And see the world at peace,
There are no children,
Crying out for food.

There is no terrorism,
And no racism too.

Then I open my eyes,
My eyes
And see the world
At war.

Glenn Young (13)
Dunluce School, Bushmills

I Have A Dream

I wish there were no wars,
Because they are so mad.
What are they over . . . ? Nothing.
Stupid wee things
Or just people being sad.

Young lives being killed for nothing.
Terrorists killing for revenge
Predestined just for greed.
Others are acting hard.
If there were no wars, fewer people would die.

Why can't people just be happy with what they have,
Instead of starting a war over oil?
And let people have their own countries,
And if they decide to kill each other,
Then let them get on with it.

You think it's so hard
But you don't see what it's doing
To the soldiers' families, they are being so hurt.
Just think about it for a minute,
Then you'll see why there should be no war.

Charlotte O'Neill (13)
Dunluce School, Bushmills

I Have A Dream

I have a dream,
That I am a goldfish in a stream.
I want to get out,
But I just can't shout.
I swim up and down,
But I can't make a sound.
My day is so long,
And my nights feel so wrong.
No one can see me,
Oh, how I want to be free!

Stephanie Dunlop (13)
Dunluce School, Bushmills

I Have A Dream

I dream I am a star,
Away up, up far.
I dream I am a fish,
Away in the sea, that's my wish.

I dream I am lots of things,
But who knows what life brings.
I dream I am really good,
'Cause I know I really should.

I dream I am the best,
But I know I'm like the rest.
I dream, you can see,
What I really want to be.

I dream, I dream, I dream.

Clare Gault (13)
Dunluce School, Bushmills

I Have A Dream

D aisies low on the ground,
R ainbows high in the sky
E verything is all around me
A lways near beside me
M any stars I see at night
S weet dreams and goodnight.

Ashleigh McCracken (13)
Dunluce School, Bushmills

I Have A Dream

I wish there was no starvation in far-out countries,
I hope everyone will be one
And one day come together as one
And not have to worry anymore.

My life would be much better if I knew alive or dead
I would still be in everyone's hearts forever . . .

I pray for those we have loved,
That we will treasure for the rest of our days . . .
I pray!

Elizabeth Aiken (12)
Dunluce School, Bushmills

I Have A Dream

I have a dream
To help me cope with anything
If you could see the world of a fairy tale
You are the only thing I think about each day.

There's no need for greed or hunger
Or being selfish to family or friends.
Just imagine living in peace
Wouldn't there be a lot?

I have a dream
To help me cope with anything
If you could see the wonder of a fairy tale
You are the only thing I think about each day.

Esme Christie (12)
Dunluce School, Bushmills

I Have A Dream

That all harm will go away
That people can go out and play
And hunger will stay away.
Drugs will not be used.
Homeless will have homes.
Wars will end.
Death no problem.

Life not wasted.
Jobs are in plenty.
Global warming stops.
People will share.
To be happy is the way of life.
No religion too.
No greed!

Kyle Collins (12)
Dunluce School, Bushmills

I Have A Dream

I have a dream
that my life will not end.
I have a dream
that you'll always be my friend.
I have a dream
that my family will never get hurt.
I have a dream
about all the boys who flirt!

Chloe Young (12)
Dunluce School, Bushmills

I Have A Dream

Why are there people fighting in Iraq,
people killing for no reason?
People being killed in cold blood.
Why can't we just stop and see
how much better it could be?

Calum Johnston (14)
Dunluce School, Bushmills

Stop Racism

I've just moved house
I came from South Africa
My name in Michael
Sometimes I'm scared to go to school,
I'm always beat up there.
I was beat up one day in school.
I only have one friend, he sticks up for me a lot
But my dream is to stop racism
For me and other kids.

Thomas Gamble (12)
Dunluce School, Bushmills

Millions

Dreaming of being a millionaire
Dreaming of a big house
With a swimming pool
A wardrobe full of clothes
Being able to go shopping every day
I have a dream to be a *millionaire!*

Rachel Collins (12)
Dunluce School, Bushmills

Who Will Care?

I'm all alone.
No way to be found.
I sit in this cage,
All by myself.
No one will know,
No one will care.
I am the last,
The last of my kind.
We all have a dream,
A wish or a wonder
That someone will rescue me
From this horrible place.

Daniel McKee (12)
Dunluce School, Bushmills

I Have A Dream

I would love to go to America,
Where the fantasy all begins.
The dream castle in Disneyland,
Where I would love to go in.
The rides, the fun, the laughter.
I wish I was there.
One day I'll go,
My family and I
Wait until you see,
With your own two eyes.

Delan Akyol (12)
Dunluce School, Bushmills

Black Subaru

I have a dream
I hope it comes true
That some day I'll be able
To drive a black Subaru.
I could go many places
And come back when I please
I might even get to go
To some far away races.
I know if I keep trying
My dream will come true
And in a few more years
I'll be driving a black Subaru.

Dwayne Hussey (15)
Elmbrook Special School, Enniskillen

I Have A Dream

A dream of hope
A dream of change
A dream of peace

For I want my children to grow up in a perfect world.
A world free of war and hatred.

Even on the darkest day
If you believe there will be light.

Even if there is no hope
If you believe everything will become better.

Believe in yourself
Believe in the people around you.

I have a dream.

Believe.

Ashley Parkinson (13)
Foxhills Technology College, Scunthorpe

I Have A Dream

Oh I have a dream
To wipe the slate clean
Like water running down a stream.

If there was a machine
That could make things clean
It would make the world a better place
And put a smile upon my face.

With the black and the white separate
The world is dull
But when they are together it is brighter.

So bring them together
Like birds of a feather
And leave them alone forever.

David Smith (13)
Foxhills Technology College, Scunthorpe

I Have A Dream

I have a dream
That in the future I could say my last goodbye to my nanna.

I have a dream
That in the future people in Africa
Could have a better life than they do now.

I have a dream
That in the future criminals will pay for their crime
Whatever they have done.

I have a dream
That in the future animal cruelty will stop
So there are more animals to see.

I have a dream
That in the future we will have peace in our world.

I have a dream today.

Emma Cox (13)
Foxhills Technology College, Scunthorpe

I Have A Dream

I have a dream that the world is laid on a beautiful, fluffy cloud,
I have a dream that death does not, and never will exist,
I have a dream that cruelty, and unpleasantness
was never introduced to the world,
I have a dream that happiness and unselfishness
is stretched in every corner by every wall,
I have a dream that laughter is spread upon everyone existing,
I have a dream that my children, and other children
can live in this dream,
I have a dream where everyone is free,
Free from cruelty, from racism, from mankind threatening our lives,
I have a dream that the world can hold hands
with friendship and rapturousness,
I have a dream, where guns, wars, knives and weapons
are banished around the Earth,
I have a dream that from today,
everyone can live their lives in cheerfulness,
I have a dream, a dream that could change everyone's life
from misery to gleefulness,
I want my dream to start and never finish, to never, ever end.

Freddie Connal (12)
Foxhills Technology College, Scunthorpe

I Have A Dream

I magine the dreams that you have.

H ere in your mind's eye
A ll the things that you can do
V ery little criminals left
E veryone is safe in the world.

A dream you could never have imagined.

D reams that you are the boss
R eal life things about your dreams
E ven if you don't think it is happening
A ll dreams come true
M e and my mates' dreams come true.

Scott Cowling (13)
Foxhills Technology College, Scunthorpe

I Have A Dream

I have a dream that I will see your face again
Looking for me standing alone,
You look like the same way you died
The way you wanted to be.
I see you standing there,
Your face so light, those beautiful golden hazel brown eyes,
Your pink, luscious, sparkling lips
Your black shiny hair over your face
Just the way you like it.
I remember your smell, your scent takes me into Heaven
I shout your name then you take my hand,
But this will never happen, you're gone, never coming back
I know you will be waiting for me when my time is up.
This is my dream.
RIP Will.

Lauren Cowling (13)
Foxhills Technology College, Scunthorpe

When I Dance

When I dance I gleam and shine
My body tingles all the time
I twist and shake to the beat
I spin and twirl and move my feet.

Dancing makes me feel so enthusiastic
This is because it's so fantastic
I feel like I am Mariah Carey
But when I'm on stage it feels so scary.

Performing is totally me
I work the music for people to see
The costumes are my favourite things
They glitter and shimmer when my body swings.

April Whitehead (11)
Hope High School, Salford

Originality

Originality is the key to success
From what you watch on TV
To the way that you dress

Another kid at school says to you,
'Hey look at this phone,'
Will you buy one too?

The other girls wear ponytails
But you have your hair loose
It blows ships' sails.

The other people like Jacqueline Wilson
But good old Charles Dickens
Is your true inspiration

You can be creative, you can be smart
But you're one in six billion
Just follow your own heart.

Teigan Mason (12)
Hope High School, Salford

One In A Million

In times of darkness and fear
And in a sea of deep despair and destruction
It only takes one shining star
To the clear the darkness and eradicate the fear
Throughout time and history
People have fought for their freedom
So we must be the voice of those who cannot speak
The ears of those who cannot hear
The arms of those who cannot take action
The world is a sick place
People die like the inevitability of raindrops in Britain
For no apparent reason
So stand up and take action
For those who need help and action.

Josh Blakeley (14)
Hope High School, Salford

Feel

What inspires me,
Is the ability to feel.
No matter what it is,
Fantasy or real.

The way the sun shines,
And keeps you warm in the day.
Or the way the stars sparkle,
So I just like to say . . .

'Tonight is a night I'll never forget,
The moon is full and bright.
Just tell me I'm here, I'm alive,
And everything will be alright.'

When someone tells me I'm special,
It makes me laugh and smile.
So then I feel happiness,
And it won't go away for a while.

And when that happens . . .
I'll be sad again.
But it'll happen once more,
And soon feel the same.

- The way you feel is important . . .
Just smile, it's worth it -

Feel the way you want to
And soon when the sadness is shown in your heart,
In your mind you'll know it won't last long.
Cherish special moments in your life.

Emily Johnson (14)
Hope High School, Salford

My Hero

I have a dream
To live like my grandad
For many years.
Living for a century
Living life to the full.
The bravest and the most exciting guy I ever met
He loves me and I know he does
He used to cater for us.
He told me later, treated me with respect
And I treated him the same way
Even though my life is not perfect.
He made me the person I am right now
He lived for his family.
When we have a gathering.
He is the most important man in the family.
He is our knight in shining armour.
The perfect man.
My hero.
And I know he is going to leave us soon
He inspires me to make the most of life.

Bolaji Fagbure (13)
Hope High School, Salford

My Inspiration

My inspiration is my best friend,
I read the message she always sends
She cheers me up when I am down
She makes me laugh,
She makes me frown.
I can trust her with anything,
She tells me things that can be interesting.
She's really funny,
Sometimes silly.
At the end of the day she's Keighley,

My best friend.

Abby Byrne (13)
Hope High School, Salford

Dreams

At night my mind wants to explore,
My dreams are what I most adore!

With bouncing bunnies and slithering snakes
And lunatic lions that live in lakes!

Running through tunnels that lead to the park,
See dogs that miaow and cats that bark!

People rolling down hills and into bushes,
Falling from the sky in great big gushes!

Flying your aeroplane so high in the sky,
Waiting for the day that it crashes and you die!

Vampires creeping around in the night,
Sneaking up and giving you a nasty bite!

With nightmares where back to sleep is the hardest place to go,
Mine were always about someone trying to cut off my big toe!

Although on Earth these may never come true,
In my mind these dreams were true!

Emily Grech (12)
Hope High School, Salford

Poem About My Mum

My mum inspires me because she's always got a sparkling smile
And a happy face to see
She encourages me in everything I do
She puts her arm around me
When tears fall down my face
She's always there to dry them
And makes me smile again.

Jasmine Bailey (13)
Hope High School, Salford

A Poem About My Mum

My mum encourages me,
in everything I do.
She always makes me happy
with her happy, smiley face.
She is always working very hard
in work and at home.
I can always turn to my mum
when I need help or get things wrong
and her caring words make everything better.
My mum!

Rebecca Hart (13)
Hope High School, Salford

Dian Fossey

Trekking through the jungle
Following a nearly faint cry . . .
A baby maybe?
Finding a baby orang-utan,
Holding its dead mother's finger
Inspecting the baby. Is it alright?
Lifting the baby away from its mother
Frightened.
Holding it in your arms
Taking the mother and baby back to camp
Burying its mother, saying goodbye.
Frightened.
The baby suckles on a bottle of milk
Being a surrogate mother to the orang-utan
Giving it a name
The baby grows up. Setting it free.
It glances back
As if saying goodbye.
My inspiration.

Keighley Sheldon (13)
Hope High School, Salford

Kelly C - The Superstar

An average child, parents divorced,
She thought that her life was cursed.
To end in sadness but wait and see,
For the star she was about to be.

At first her dream job to be,
Was a marine explorer under the sea.
But scary films made her understand,
That she was meant to stay on land.

Her friend inspired her to go
To put her talent on a show.
Achieving every girl's ambition,
Trying her hardest she did an audition.

In her heart she really knew,
This was what she was meant to do.
After all the misery, sadness and hate,
Kelly had done it, she'd found her fate.

Kim Rawlinson (14)
Hope High School, Salford

A Help Of Her Friend

Her wrists are red.
The tears she cries
Show the suffering in her life.
She has no one.
Her soul is black and dead.

Her friend is helping her,
Picking her up,
Making her feel like someone.

Friends. Help is like a diamond,
Bright and shiny
And helps you through your life's journey.

Poppy Gabrielides (13)
Hope High School, Salford

My Haikus

These are my haikus,
They tell who inspires me
And it is just me.

The inspiration,
It's in me, it's loads of things,
It's an energy.

The inspiration,
Pushes me to do my best,
Puts me to the test.

The inspiration,
It's an invisible force
It keeps me on course.

The inspiration,
Will help me when I'm older
To get a good job.

For now it is just
Pushing me through school, college,
Then to that last goal.

Leighton Lawson (14)
Hope High School, Salford

Kelly Clarkson

Who could have known that life is like a wheel?
Sometimes you're down,
Sometimes you're up,
The hardness and sadness,
Happiness is the exchange.

If you try and try,
Success will always be behind you,
Just like Kelly . . .
She may be from a broken family
But that doesn't matter . . .
She faced the reality
And never gave up . . .

Dreaming of being a marine biologist,
But 'Jaws' . . . the film . . .
Put her off,
She worked after high school,
Pharmacy assistant, telemarketer,
Comedy club cocktail waitress.

Despite all the hardship
A moment that will change her life
Has come at last . . .
Her best friend believes in her . . .
Trust and respect
Are the most important in life . . .

A million albums sold!
She is blessed!
Blessed for not giving up
Blessed for trying
Blessed for believing that,
Everything is possible
And blessed for being strong

From a normal teenage girl in Texas,
Now a famous singer and actress in Hollywood

A moment like this
Some people wait for a lifetime
But for Kelly . . .
It's an opportunity . . .
Opportunity that could
Change her life
Change.

Lovely Lobeda (14)
Hope High School, Salford

Motivation

Motivation, an invisible force inside you
Makes you do good things,
Makes you do bad things
That leave you feeling happy,
Things that leave you feeling sad.
Motivation, a powerful force inside you
That makes you do what you do.

Xennon Gee (14)
Hope High School, Salford

My Living Nightmare

I have a dream,
Of a clear blue stream,
Reflecting the sun's golden beam.
Where children play,
Day after day,
Where the daffodils gently sway.

I have a dream,
Where the blossoms fly,
With the birds and the clouds in the sky,
Where the people laze,
In a daze,
Where the animals happily graze.

I have a dream,
A dream of love,
Carried on the wings of a dove,
Where the sun shines bright,
Where there is no fight,
I wish for this with all my might.

I had a dream,
That turned into a nightmare,
Where famine roamed across the land,
Where litter ruined our lovely sand.

I had a dream,
That turned into a nightmare,
Where people didn't care,
Where people didn't share.

I had a dream,
That turned into a nightmare,
With never-ending war,
And everyone so poor.

I had a dream,
That turned into a nightmare,
The colour of the world was grey,
This is the world today.

Stephanie Carter (12)
King William's College, Isle of Man

I Have A Dream

I have a dream that fighting will stop
And not make people feel on top.
No more hitting or punching in the face,
Not making everything seem like a race.

I have a dream that bullying will end,
And people will learn how to borrow or lend.
No more tormenting or calling people names,
But people having fun and playing games.

I have a dream that wars will cease,
I wish the world would cultivate peace.
I have a dream that people won't fight,
And one day these people together will unite.

Camilla Brahde (12)
King William's College, Isle of Man

I Have A Dream

I have a dream,
A horrible one,
Where tears are coming down in a stream.

I have a dream,
A sociable one,
Where the city shines with a gleam.

I have a dream,
Where children would frolic in green fields
But they can't because of a war-like scream.

I have a dream,
To be the best,
To build my self-esteem.

Louis Porter (14)
King William's College, Isle of Man

I Have A Dream

It seems to me my only friends
Are the moon, animals and sun.
The humans don't seem to care
About what they have done.

I'm struggling now to survive,
In 50 years I will die
Because of the humans.

I'm getting so annoyed now
About the pollution,
So volcanoes are erupting,
When there's a really simple solution.

Walk a little further,
Drive a little less,
Everything will be OK
And the world won't be a mess.

This can be achieved
Easy peasy 1, 2, 3
So why don't do you do it?
I'm the world, so save me.

Alana Kennedy (12)
King William's College, Isle of Man

I Have A Dream

I have a dream that there would be no global warming.
I have a dream that there will be no terrorists.
I have a dream school will be fun.
I have a dream that my family will live forever.
I have a dream my grandparents come back to life.
I have a dream the world can be a better place.

Kris Novak (12)
King William's College, Isle of Man

I Have A Dream

I have a dream
That not too far ahead in time
The world will see no crime

I have a dream
Man's inhumanity to man
Will no longer be the plan

I have a dream
That good things can happen for us all
If we can stand and do not fall

I have a dream
Not to make victims to all that's bad
Just pray for the lonely and the sad

I have a dream
That just for one day
Fear and poverty will go away

I have a dream
We will live with each other
And everyone will be our brother.

Bradley Kitt (14)
King William's College, Isle of Man

I Have A Dream

I have a dream,
Of a world of peace,
Where happiness reigns
And will never cease.

I have a dream,
Of no poverty,
Where no one is poor,
Or very hungry.

I have a dream,
Of a land without greed,
Where everyone shares
And no one's in need.

I have a dream,
Of animals free.
Not caged up,
For people to see.

I have a dream,
Of streets without litter,
Where everything's clean
And all is a-glitter.

I have a dream,
Of no pollution,
Where nothing is killed,
Because of our nation.

I have a nightmare,
Of what the future could be,
If we don't work together,
To save our country.

I have a challenge,
For every person;
To make our world better,
Before it can worsen.

Maeve McCarney (12)
St Mary's Grammar School, Magherafelt

I Have A Dream

I have a dream that I will be
A pirate sailing round the sea,
A drummer rocking in a band,
But the pain would be left in my hand.

I have a dream that I will be
A hairdresser with a cheap fee,
A HE teacher who makes lovely buns
But then the children would all weigh tonnes.

I have a dream that I will be
A postlady doing my delivery,
But the dog across the road would bark at me
I'd have a hole in my clothes and everyone would see.

I have a dream that I will be
The first person ever to see
The sun collide with the moon,
I'd be making money pretty soon.

I have a dream that when I grow up
I'll get to go to the World Cup,
And even though I don't like football
It will still be the best adventure of all.

I have a dream that when I grow up
I'll get to have my own pup,
Then maybe I'll be a vet
Or help people to choose their pet.

I have a dream to be
The person I call *me*.

Catherine Scullion (12)
St Mary's Grammar School, Magherafelt

I Have A Dream

I have a dream,
Where smiles beam.
Where the sky is blue
And where people don't have a clue.

I have a dream,
Or so it seems.
Is it all real,
It's time to reveal.

I have a dream,
Where the sun can gleam.
Where the world lives in peace
And prisoners are all released.

I have a dream,
Where no one screams.
Where children clap
And also tap.

I have a dream,
Where we are a team.
A great big family,
That lives happily.

I have a dream,
A great big dream.
When I think, it makes me gleam.

Declan Averell (12)
St Mary's Grammar School, Magherafelt

I Have A Dream

I have a dream,
But will it come true?
When there aren't complaints
In a never-ending queue.

I have a dream,
When everything's better,
When not everything is sold
On the Internetter!

I have a dream,
When things are dead,
Like sadness and worry
And hatred and dread.

I have a dream,
Where the world is bright,
It is quite possible
If we do what is right.

If we work together,
Things could be great.
We must make a change
Before it's too late.

Enda Boorman (12)
St Mary's Grammar School, Magherafelt

I Have A Dream

I have a dream
I have a dream of a world
A peaceful world
Tropical skies, emerald blades of grass
Freedom

I have a dream
I have a dream of a dove
A white, pure, silent dove
Free of war and prejudice
Peace

I have a dream
I have a dream of a cloud
An opal whirl floating through a clear blue sky
It won't turn black and rain down on our already ruined world
Purity

I have a dream
I have a dream of the sun
A bright yellow sun
A splendid fire burning, burning in the garden of redemption
Light

I have a dream
I have a dream about people
People, wandering through the wilderness of time
No arguments, wars, no racism, hatred
Love

I have a dream
I have a dream of freedom and peace
Of purity, light
Of love
When will my dreams come true?

Bríd Mackle (12)
St Mary's Grammar School, Magherafelt

I Have A Dream

I have a dream that everyone will be united,
Proud of whom they are and free,
I have a dream that everyone will be unique
And not judged on how they see.

They will become a nation,
And not be torn apart.
They will be seen for who they are,
And what is in their heart.

They won't be judged on difference
Such as the colour of the skin,
They won't be judged on religion
And what they think within.

They will not feel so lonely,
They will feel as if they're good,
They will feel the thoughts of a person,
And the way they really should.

They were judged on how they look,
And laws were put in place,
They even got discriminated,
By the colour of their face.

I hope that they will solve their problems,
Of which turned them away.
Their happiness finally came to them,
When one stood up and had their say.

Richard Moorhead (12)
The Wallace High School, Lisburn

Climate Change

A deadly blanket,
A choking planet,
A melting country,
A planet going to extremes.

Sweltering summers,
Freezing winters,
One planet taking psychos.

We must stop,
Stop pumping these deadly gasses,
Pumping them into a thermolating blanket,
That will one day kill us all.

Ian Nelson (12)
The Wallace High School, Lisburn

A Better World For Me Would Be . . .

When poverty is ended
When racism erased
When sectarianism is gone
When cancer can be cured
When world hunger is refrained
When animal cruelty is stopped
And when French is removed from schools!
This is my dream

Hannah Nash (12)
The Wallace High School, Lisburn

I Have A Dream!

I have a dream . . .
That one day people will be treated with respect.
I have a dream . . .
That people will not be discriminated for their race,
religion or the colour of their skin and even the colour of their hair.
I have a dream . . .
That people will donate more to the Third World because
people are dying and we can stop it if we would just try to help
I have a dream . . .
That no one will be left out and that people will not judge
so quickly and give people who are different, a chance as they
didn't choose their colour or race and they don't kick up a fuss
about white people so why should we be so discriminating?
I have a dream . . .
That one day all this will sink in and the people who are
being racist and discriminating will stop and listen to everyone
else's views and opinions because we can't live in a world with
all of these fights and discrimination because it is horrible and
unnecessary.
I have a dream . . .
That one day everyone will understand that this is not right
and it is unfair and once that happens we will live in a much better
world but until it happens we will keep trying!

Jennifer McDowell (12)
The Wallace High School, Lisburn

My Dream - Haikus

Just imagine if
The world was friendly and fun,
And it wasn't bad.

Just imagine if
The world wasn't depressing,
And it was happy.

Just imagine if
The world was joyful and bright,
And it wasn't dull.

Just imagine if
The world was interesting,
Rather than boring.

Just imagine if
The world was good and helpful,
Rather than unkind.

Just imagine if
My dream of a perfect world,
Finally came true.

Ruth Patterson (12)
The Wallace High School, Lisburn

Poverty

How sad I feel when I see,
Hungry and starving children from poor countries,
I feel ashamed because I have so much.
Let every family that can, send food and clothes,
To make these people have a better life.
This will only help them for a while,
We need to help them grow their own crops,
So that their future will be more secure,
And they can make a life for themselves.
So in the future when I turn on the TV,
I will not see scared and empty faces looking at me.
But children running and having fun,
When their crops grow in the sun.

Andy Neely (12)
The Wallace High School, Lisburn

I Have A Dream

I have a dream,
For no more homework,
For the freedom of the mind.
No more homework,
For imaginative capture.
No more homework,
For relaxation and peace.
No more homework,
For better grades.
No more homework,
For no more boredom.
No more homework,
For the lease of life!

Neil Mulholland (12)
The Wallace High School, Lisburn

World Hunger

I have a dream that world hunger can end.
That the bitter pain the Third World suffers can descend
And no man has to worry about his family dying from hunger.

I have a dream that everyone is equal
Every nation can stand up for themselves.
I believe everyone deserves a chance
To do something in their life.
This is my goal and this is my dream
So all the world has something to mean.

Boyd Rodgers (12)
The Wallace High School, Lisburn

I Have A Dream

The world would be a better place
If there wasn't such a thing as expense.
Prices make the world so much harder.
You can't get things you need because of it.
Poor people basically die of starvation.
If I could only just change this,
Life would be so much better.
It would be amazing,
Nobody ever going hungry,
People all living longer.
It would all be great fun
And everybody would be happy.
Just think of all the stuff you could do.
Travelling all around the world,
Living in a massive house,
Having heaps of jewellery.
Imagine being able to afford anything you ever wanted.
Imagine all your wishes coming true.
Imagine, the world would never be the same again.

Stephen Murray (12)
The Wallace High School, Lisburn

My Dream

A beautiful world is what I see in my dreams.
Where orang-utans are safe to be
In the forests, free from danger!

Their homes are safe and so are their lives,
And a stop to poaching for which I strive,
And the forests free from danger!

Today, poachers kill freely,
Making money from fur,
And now, about this, I will not hear,
I want forests free from danger!

Palm oil growing destroys the trees,
The orang-utans' homes are ruined,
And to all of these treacheries,
I want to put an end.
I want forests free from danger!

Rainforests are being cut down all the time,
Animals and their homes are dead,
But the people who do this don't really care,
And I have these words to be said:
I want forests free from danger!

Ollie Rusk (12)
The Wallace High School, Lisburn

I Have A Dream

I have a dream,
That no one has had before,
Someone will come ringing,
Or knocking at my door.

'Peace is all around us'
They will come and say,
'Everyone is singing songs
In a pleasant and cheerful way.'

I have a dream,
That wars will suddenly stop,
That people will hold hands,
And down the road they'll hop.

The sounds of bombs will vanish,
There will be no explosions outside my door,
My dream is vivid,
That there will be peace for evermore.

I have a dream that the sun will come out,
That people will be happy,
And none will give a shout.

All wars will stop,
Of this I am sure,
And all the wounds and cuts,
Will suddenly be cured.

My dream will happen,
Today or tomorrow,
But right now,
My heart is full of sorrow.

Amy Stephens (12)
The Wallace High School, Lisburn

I Have A Dream

I have a dream,
This dream is not my own,
It is shared by thousands,
Remember you are not alone.

Black or white,
Fat or thin,
Everyone is different,
Although it is the same world we are in.

Bullies are about,
They beat up everyone,
For being too smart,
Or designing a piece of art.

Poverty in Africa,
It's not fair this takes place,
Because the government is greedy,
They cannot share their money to dying people.

People die because they are black,
Those who don't die slave,
Black people are known to be brave,
They get bullied and don't fight back.

Katie McKnight (12)
The Wallace High School, Lisburn

My Dream

Weighed down by chains is the world,
Until the key of peace appears,
It is as an angel, it comes slowly,
It unlocks the chains with a shining key
And the chains of war are removed,

Peace and freedom abound,
Like unlocked shackles, the chains of war disappear,
No more weeping, no more dying,
The world enters a new era,
Of peace of prosperity,
This is my dream.

Neil Ross (12)
The Wallace High School, Lisburn

If I Could Change The World

If I could change the world,
Then cars there would not be
So everybody could walk
And healthier they would be.

No more nasty traffic jams,
The buses could run free
For people who must travel far
And walking could not be.

Little boy racers
Do definitely kill.
Deaths on the road
Would be practically nil.

Saving our natural resources
Keeping the environment clean,
Can only help in the future
To save our plants and trees.

The planet would be safer,
No fumes roaming free
People would breathe easy
And asthma there would not be.

Glenn Reid (12)
The Wallace High School, Lisburn

I Have A Dream

I have a dream
That poverty would be history

Children dying
People crying

Shouting for help
And getting no answer back

Wells being built
But not enough

Children on the streets
And look at us with our proper homes

Parents dying
And children being left alone

Children working in the fields
Not able to afford school

There's poverty in this world
But why?

Because we can't
Be bothered to help.

Nicola Millar (12)
The Wallace High School, Lisburn

My Dream For The Future

My dream would be this,
All the governments and presidents,
That make big lists,
Of finances and debts would listen.
If they would listen carefully,
The world would change completely,
This would be the answer and the key,
To a new way of living,
For you and me.
All the debts to dissolve,
How they all could resolve,
Poverty, hunger and greed.
So they can sow their own seed
And set themselves free.

Jack Morton (12)
The Wallace High School, Lisburn

I Have A Dream

I have a dream,
For all the world,
To live in perfect harmony,
No more guns and no more wars.
Free from pain and suffering,
All people will be equal,
Famine and disease will cease,
Children will roam safely
And play hand in hand,
We will care more for our Earth
And keep it pollution free.
What a bright future there would be,
If my dream became reality!

Emma Patterson (11)
The Wallace High School, Lisburn

I Am What I Am

I am what I am
Why can't you see?
I cannot be what you want me to be.
I am what I am
And I'm proud of it too,
Catholic, Protestant, Muslim or Jew.
I am what I am
I cannot change,
It hurts me to think that I am strange.
I am what I am
I'm just like you,
Skin colour shouldn't matter, but it does to you.
I am what I am
What do you want me to do?
I'm not going to leave because you told me to.
I am what I am
Stop harassing me,
It's not my fault, why can't you see?
I am what I am
God made me this way,
Stop calling me names every night and day.
I am what I am
And that's all I can be.
I am what I am
So let me be me.

Megan Rooney (12)
The Wallace High School, Lisburn

I Have A Dream

I have a dream,
That no man can destroy,
No man, no woman,
No girl, no boy.

My dream is equality,
That man can sit daily with each other,
Like sister with sister,
And brother with brother.

Racism will be gone within this day,
If you just listen to what I have to say,
Happiness will be found in every man,
If we hope and do the best we can.

I will achieve all that I can,
But I only have the power of one man,
Join together, we will play this game,
So that nobody has to live in shame.

I believe in something new,
I have hope and faith in all I do,
I only have the power of one man,
So join with me, we'll do all we can.

This is my dream, this is my goal,
We can overcome this and take control,
We'll have more family; we'll have more friends,
So altogether now we *will* make amends.

Vicky Slaine (12)
The Wallace High School, Lisburn

I Dream

I dream of a world with nothing but love,
I dream of a world with nothing but hope,
I dream of a world with nothing but kindness,
But most of all I dream of peace,
No death, no illness, no tragedy,
You won't get this in war,
What you will get is a world without love and hope,
A world with nothing but pain,
A nasty world of fear,
A world with pure hatred, sin and defiance,
So please just avoid the war,
This is my dream.

Marcus Sarre (12)
The Wallace High School, Lisburn

War

The plotting of an assassination,
The conflict and violence between the nations.
The worry and terror of life deduction,
The vast amount of all the destruction.
The grief of loss dwells,
The memories of those murderous hells.
The terrorism in the city,
The world that ran out of pity.
All this killing, all this gore,
Is caused by man, is caused by war.

Alex Philpot (12)
The Wallace High School, Lisburn

I Have A Dream

My poem is about global poverty.
In hundreds of countries it is changing lives
It is happening in countries such as Africa.
People are dying every day from it.

If richer countries like the USA and Great Britain,
Would donate more money to poverty affected countries.
It would make a huge difference to all the poverty hit countries.

A man from Malawi called Hudson came to my church.
He talked to all the congregation about living in Africa,
And about just how poor Malawi really is.

If you lived in a poverty affected country
You would have little if any weekly income,
And also it is a very poor style of life.

If you were a farmer you would farm barren land.
If there was a drought,
You couldn't farm the land.

The dying people of Africa and other poor countries,
Do really need your help,
So why not donate some money?

David Mckerr (12)
The Wallace High School, Lisburn

I Have A Dream

I have a dream
That a football shirt won't mean a thing
That everyone would be thought of the same
If Rangers or Celtic or whatever their game.

I have a dream
That everyone would be treated the same
That the old won't be compared to the young
And the poor won't be laughed at by the rich
But can join hands together as one.

I have a dream
That someday racism will stop
That humans can be like a herd of horses
All colours, shapes and sizes
That they could graze side by side
Proud to be different.

I have a dream
That this poem will be remembered
And someday this dream may come true.

Joanne Leathem (12)
The Wallace High School, Lisburn

I Have A Dream

I have a dream that one day food and money
shall be spread evenly across the world.
No one on this Earth should need to starve to feed others.
Everyone should have an even shot in life.
All citizens of all countries no matter who they are
should have a chance to earn a salary if they wish.
All nations should be allowed to have the happiness
of health, strength and no money issues.

Daniel McCavery (12)
The Wallace High School, Lisburn

I Have A Dream To End All Poverty

P oor people squashed into a tiny mud hut, hot and thirsty.
O ur semis, bungalows and mansions packed
  with our showers and televisions.
V arious diseases that can be cured lurk in their short water supply.
E very Diet Coke and coffee sipped without a single thought.
R unning out of wheat and crops, here there're Mace shops.
T ummies gurgle after endless hot meals,
  we don't know how hunger feels.
Y ou and I keep them poor to have the life that we prefer.

Helen Lavery (12)
The Wallace High School, Lisburn

I Have A Dream

I have a dream, that one day there will no poverty,
No people discriminating the Third World,
Poor people can get help for their own safety
And eat all the food they want.

I have a dream that disease will die,
No death from AIDS or cancer or starvation,
These people deserve the best
And one day say goodbye to the sadness left behind.

I have a dream that dirty water will be clean,
No food will be lots of food,
Dreams will become reality,
The poor will become the rich.

These people may not have money,
But they have hope,
They will soon be able to do anything they want,
I'm sure they'll cope.

I have a dream,
That at the end of time
The poor will be the rich
And the famous shall be unknown.

Paul Maguire (12)
The Wallace High School, Lisburn

I Have A Dream

A trigger of a gun,
The blade of a knife,
The scream of a child,
This is war.

When triggers are pulled,
When blades are stained red,
When hate is violent,
It is war.

A helpless old man,
A bleeding, wounded father,
The wailing of his son,
War brings this.

War isn't love,
War isn't victory,
But most of all,
War doesn't bring peace.

Laura Martin (12)
The Wallace High School, Lisburn

I Have a Dream

I have a dream,
That one day in the future,
We'll all just get along.
There'll be no more killings,
No more murders, no more plots,
Bomber planes will be no more,
Nor will guns or clubs,
Or swords, or spears.
No more war.
Think of the soldier,
Who could be anyone,
Living anywhere, doing anything,
Could have a wife and kids,
Not knowing if he's alive or dead,
He's likely to die without saying goodbye.
His loved ones will mourn,
Just because someone annoyed someone else.
Maybe it was all about power,
Or perhaps something quite different.
It doesn't really matter.
All I know is,
Innocent people are getting killed.
I have a dream,
Of world peace.

Jonathon McMurray (12)
The Wallace High School, Lisburn

Wars

I have a dream that one day there will be never be any wars . . .
No deaths from wars,
No sadness from friends and family,
No blood from the battleground.
I have a dream that one day there will never be any wars.

I have a dream that everyone will get along together
And there will be no need for any wars,
Everyone will agree on a solution,
Everyone will be friends,
Everyone in the world will get along
And it will be a nice and peaceful place to live in,
I have a dream that one day there will never be any wars, full stop!

Sarah McCallan (12)
The Wallace High School, Lisburn

I Have A Dream

I have a dream that one day there will be no fighting.
I have a dream that there will be no world hunger.
I have a dream that everyone will get along.
I have a dream that there will be no more hate.
I have a dream that no one will ever kill.
I have a dream that it doesn't matter how rich you are
                              to have a good life.
I have a dream that there will be no more murder.
I have a dream that there will be no more slavery.
I have a dream that everyone will love each other.
I have a dream.

Jordan McMullen (12)
The Wallace High School, Lisburn

A Dream Of Peace

It must be an awful life, for the one you are name calling,
Abusing to amuse yourself.
You just don't think
How the other feels, and you have no real reason for hurting them so.
Do you?

I can honestly say that I wouldn't want to be in that person's shoes,
To be used like a doormat,
For people to wipe their nasty comments on.
Would you?

'Let freedom ring'. These are the famous words of Martin Luther King.
Let equality fill the Earth.
'Why should we all be equal?' you say,
But then again,
Why not?

Victoria Lilley (12)
The Wallace High School, Lisburn

Animal Dream

A bolish dog fights and
N ever leave pit bulls
I n mindless rages that the
M aleficent
A bominations that bred them
L eave them in.

D eath to hunting and
R epulsive
E xperiments and chemical testing on
A nimals, which deserve freedom from
M onstrous hunters.

William Martin (12)
The Wallace High School, Lisburn

This Was Martin Luther King

He did so much
He freed so many
He helped them all

This was Martin Luther King.

He was despised
He was hated
He was murdered

This was Martin Luther King.

He went through so much
He was as brave as a lion
But all to save humanity

This was Martin Luther King.

He was freedom personified
He loved everyone
This was Martin Luther King.

Iain McAleavey (12)
The Wallace High School, Lisburn

Equality

Think about equality.
It isn't just a word,
It isn't just a saying,
It isn't just a phrase,
Think about equality.

Think about equality.
It has a true meaning,
For fairness, for balance,
For equivalence, for sameness,
Think about equality.

Think about equality.
For everyone is equal,
Everyone is the same,
Everyone has a fair chance,
Equality.

Joanne McConnell (12)
The Wallace High School, Lisburn

World Peace Poem

I have a dream that one day . . .
The starving mouths of Africa are fed
That the hunger not the people be dead.
The people of Africa must not drool
As the people of Britain stuff their mouths so full.

I have a dream . . .
That there is no more fighting anymore
That all weapons are thrown out the door.
That no one gets killed or dies
And gets eaten by the flies.

I have a dream . . .
That everyone is equal
That everyone is fed
That there is no more fighting
But peace throughout the world.

Alastair McCracken (12)
The Wallace High School, Lisburn

I Have A Dream . . .

I have a dream . . .

That peace will be reunited,
No longer will there be violence,
Black and white and Muslim and Hindu,
Will be brought into harmony,
And the world will be a friendly place to live.

I have a dream . . .

That poverty will be extinct,
Hunger will never be felt,
There will be an endless supply of clean water,
And that black, white, Muslim and Hindu
Will have the same education.

I have a dream . . .

Hannah McConkey (12)
The Wallace High School, Lisburn

My Dream

M y dream is . . .
Y oung and old getting along with each other

D eath fuelled by anger being eliminated forever
R elaxing without worrying about anyone
E veryone getting along, no matter what their race or religion
A well deserved peace of mind
M y dream has been heard!

Gareth Miller (12)
The Wallace High School, Lisburn

I Have A Dream

I have a dream . . .
That there are no wars,
I have a dream . . .
That there are no more weapons.

I have a dream . . .
That everyone can be friends,
I have a dream . . .
That everyone can be peaceful.

I have a dream . . .
That there is no more racism,
I have a dream . . .
That everyone is respected no matter what.

I have a dream . . .
That no one gets injured on purpose,
I have a dream . . .
That no one gets killed.

I have a dream . . .
For peace around the world!

Ryan McShannock (12)
The Wallace High School, Lisburn

My Dream For Africa

I have a dream that one day poverty will be history.
That the people in Africa will have plenty of food and water.
That the rain will come and the famine will go away.
That the fields will grow plenty of food to eat.
That hunger will cease and plenty will reign.
The cattle will graze in the field and will be healthy at last.
That there will be doctors in the little village
to cure all diseases and sickness.
That the people in Africa will have enough money
to buy food and clothes.
That everyone will be happy,
This is my dream for Africa!

Andrew McGrath (12)
The Wallace High School, Lisburn

I Have A Dream

I have a dream that one day all nations,
be them small or big can live together in peace.
To stop death and sadness.
To stop fear and bombs.
To help rebuild buildings - not flatten them.
I have a dream that one day
someone would stop and think about families
who have lost loved ones.
To talk and sort out problems -
without guns or bullets.
'To live in peace is something we take for granted,
for others it's something they dream about every night'.

Adam Matthews (12)
The Wallace High School, Lisburn

I Have A Dream

P overty is an awful thing because people in Africa
   and places like that have no food or water.
O pen your eyes to the effect of poverty on the world
V ery often this happens because the people
   don't have any homes, families or clothes
E very day many people are dying across the world
R emember those who are less fortunate than you
T omorrow may never come for those who have nothing
Y ou can make a difference by giving to charity today.

Laura McCallum (12)
The Wallace High School, Lisburn

No Smoking

My dream for the world is to have no smoking
No lung disease, breathing problems or choking.

Why do people buy them?
It'll just give them problems

Their lives become short,
They are not good, any sort

They will provoke
And try to get you to smoke

It's going to kill you!
I promise this is true
If you've started and you can't stop
Stay strong and do your best!

If you've never tried this
Just give it a miss.

I know those who suffered this fate,
Take in my words before it's too late . . .

Steven McClune (12)
The Wallace High School, Lisburn

I Have A Dream

To dream, to believe
To open doors to all who don't see,
A dream which one day might come true,
A dream which you believe,
A dream worth dying for . . .
A dream, a goal, a hope, an ambition . . .
A never-ending desire . . .

This is my dream . . .

I dream of a day for all to see,
I dream about faith, I am dreaming about belief,
I dream that those children crying on the streets,
I dream, they cry no more because of what they believe,
I have seen the death, suicide, tears and bleeding . . .

No one can accept what others believe in,
The minorities, the extremists, the outcasts . . .
They all believe,
They believe in Heavens and Hells,
Higher beings and enlightenment . . .
Yet, though their beliefs are different,
One can't help but notice,
The morals are the same.

I dream of only nine words coming true . . .
'All the religions in the world are acknowledged',
That is all I dream,
But what good is a dream if only one believes?

Rosanna Lathwell (12)
The Wallace High School, Lisburn

Poverty

I have a dream that poverty be abolished from the face of the Earth.
While people with no food, no money,
No hope live under the fist of the wealthy, corrupt government.
Every day in these people's lives they live in pain,
Suffering and fear from soldiers and rebels.
These desperate people are being shot at,
Threatened and tortured silently by the government.
I have a dream that poverty can be overcome.
It will be a formidable task, but it is not impossible.
Years, even decades of money from different nations and charities.
I have a dream that the biggest dictators crumble with pressure.
While these people's dreams become realised, hopefully like mine.

Thomas Graham (12)
The Wallace High School, Lisburn

I Have A Dream

I have a dream
That one day
There will be no wars
That one day
There will be peace
That one day
The bloodshed will stop
I have a dream

I have a dream
That one day
Children can grow without racism or fear
That one day
All people will unite and be as one
That one day
Religion and colour don't divide us
I have a dream

I have a dream
That one day
We are all equal
That one day
We will all have compassion
That one day
We shall have peace
I have a dream.

Adam McAleavey (14)
The Wallace High School, Lisburn

Imagine!

War. Injustice. Poverty.
Familiar to those who have experienced them
War. Injustice. Poverty.
Familiar to those who haven't.

Peace. Justice. Prosperity.
Imagine!

Racism. Inequality. Prejudice.
We are all the same at heart
Racism. Inequality. Prejudice.
Driving us apart.

Tolerance. Equality. Acceptance.
Imagine!

No one person looks the same
Yet we share a common ground
From the fit to the lame
Just take a look around.
We can make a difference to our human ways
To conquer what sets us back,
To conquer what we lack.

Imagine!

David McCrea (14)
The Wallace High School, Lisburn

Better Together

I was walking, thinking, dreaming of a world,
A world that would work perfectly
Like a well oiled car, a world that
Would have one goal, peace.

Peace would rain down like an early dew.
All people will walk together, talk together,
Follow the same laws, worship the same God,
And all differences be put behind us.

Hurting would stop, wars would end,
All leaders to agree on things and
No more petty arguments on things to
Try and make lives easier for everyone.

If we work together, focus on our futures,
On our children's future, we will surely
Find a paradise, for everyone to work,
And live and enjoy life, for all.

And then I realised, life will never be like this,
It's what makes the world what it is,
Everyone, different views, cultures, religions,
It is what makes us unique, what makes our world unique.

Alastair McCollum (14)
The Wallace High School, Lisburn

In My World

In my world there will be,
Happiness as far as the eye could see.
Poverty will be history,
Equality won't be a mystery.

In my world people will do,
Always have a heart of true,
They will look out for one another,
And care more for each other.

In my world people
Will not have toa kill,
Not get a thrill
From causing pain.

In my world life for some won't be so hard
The starry sky like a thousand bulbs
Will not intimidate the weak,
Life shall not be so weak,
The happiness that they seek,

Shall appear.

Adam McCann (14)
The Wallace High School, Lisburn

Cast Out Your Demons

We hold in our hands,
The sword and the faith.
Waiting till it fades to day
We shall rise,
To cast out the demons,
The demons of society.

Despair, racism, violence, sectarianism,
All that we fear.
These are the hardest part of living
And we face them every day,
At school, work and play.

Now it's all upon our head,
To cast out our fears and helplessness.
It gives the weak flight,
It gives the blind sight
And society strength.

We will fight to the last light.
I mean this more than words can say.
We shall pull the plug on injustice
And set up a world of hope and equality.

Aaron McIntyre (14)
The Wallace High School, Lisburn

The Ideal World

I have a dream . . .
That rubbish wasn't a problem,
Paper used again and again.
Global warming was never heard of,
Pollution or acid rain.

I have a dream . . .
Sectarianism or racist attacks,
Were rare or obsolete.
You could walk down a road,
In a football top and not worry of being beat.

I have a dream . . .
Sweat shops were non existent.
Instead only fair trade.
The workers were treated fairly,
Less hours, less work, more paid.

I have a dream . . .
Bullies were not a problem,
No child was scared of school.
They worried about their schoolwork,
And not about being 'cool'.

I have a dream . . .
I was as free as the wind,
From the thoughts of these issues.
We're all drowning,
In the rules that we misuse.

Emma McNeice (14)
The Wallace High School, Lisburn

What I Want For The World

I have a dream,
An image, an idea,
A wish, a want,
That horror and hunger will no longer haunt.

People at home,
People away,
People belonging,
People astray.

I wish for a world,
Full of kindness and love,
Not anger and hate,
But peace from above.

I long for a world,
That's like a new planet,
No pollution or bad habits,
People acting nicely on it.

I imagine the world,
In twenty years time,
It's worse than now,
So here's my rhyme.

If we don't stop this,
Hatred and lies,
Then it's over
Right before our eyes.

I want the world to change,
I need it to,
Otherwise we're in trouble,
Please stop this, please do!

Kathryn Millen (14)
The Wallace High School, Lisburn

Dream

The world
Is dying
Children are crying
With no shoulder to cry on
Alone in their lives
Teenagers getting killed
All over knives

Innocent people thrown into jail
Murderers getting out on bail
Guns and drugs control them
They're cold and pale
Paranoia takes over
Their minds are stale

Smoke and gas
Pollute our world
Ruining futures
Ruining *now*

Stop
Why is this happening?
Why won't it stop?
Children with families
Guns and drugs control no more
The rich stop powering the poor
All badness and pain
Never again.

Laura Moore (14)
The Wallace High School, Lisburn

I Have A Dream

I have a dream in my head
That one day we will all have beds.
People to love, people to care,
And that everyone will be treated fair.

No more racism between black and white
Let people feel they have rights.
No more murders, no more hate
Let all people live their fate.

I have a dream, we all become one
Loving each other under the sun,
Giving hugs and caring for each other
For this we will all thank our brothers

In my head I just keep thinking,
What would happen if we all stop drinking?
Many of us would die and fade away
This makes me scared to think this way

I just keep dreaming everyone is equal.
No one thinking they are better than another.
If everyone would just unite together
This would make me feel so much better.

This is my dream which I hope would come true
Maybe it would help me, and also you.
So please just think what this dream could do
That is my dream from me to you.

Sophie McClean (14)
The Wallace High School, Lisburn

Hope

It's hope that can become the reality.
It's hope that fills the smile in our face.
Without it dreams cannot be made true.
It is like the breath in the bodies of our race.

For some people hope is all they have.
With hope they have power of their own.
Hope fills the hearts of many
From Japan to America to Rome.

No matter how big, no matter how small
The dreams will rise on hope alone.
The Third World people, the poor, the sick,
They will all rise up and unite.

Craig Manley (14)
The Wallace High School, Lisburn

I Have A Dream

I have a dream.
That religion doesn't matter
And people with different colour skin
Are all the same.

I have a dream.
That everyone has food,
And that there is enough for all.
Poverty does not exist.

I have a dream.
That communism exists
Around the globe
And that money is not a problem.

I have a dream.
Where rich and poor,
White and black can all play
I have a dream.

Philip Lemon (14)
The Wallace High School, Lisburn

I Have A Dream

I have dream that one day,
I will come,
Into a world,
Just built for some!

This place has a name,
Its name is Heaven,
It might have a palace,
Or even seven!

The streets will be made,
Out of pure gold,
Well they are the stories,
That I've been told.

To get to this place,
Be good, before you die,
Then you'll be lifted,
Up into the sky!

There you'll see a great person,
Who made you and me,
He even made all the stars,
In the sky you can see.

When I go there,
Where I believe,
After leaving this world,
I *will* be relieved.

Jason Kelly (14)
The Wallace High School, Lisburn

I Have A Dream

I have a dream to be Superman
Signing autographs for my number one fan.
Someday I want to fly in the sky
Everyone can watch me as I glide by.
I could even have X-ray vision
Cheat in exam papers, do no revision.
I will save the world like Spider-Man
Or fly away like Peter Pan.

I could be the Red Power Ranger
To save the world from cartoon danger.
I would have to dress in disguise
Live a life full of lies.
I could be King Kong, the gorilla
I would kill the bad guy, Godzilla.
I will be one of the Fantastic Four
Turn to fire so I can soar.
I could be one of the X-men
I don't know how and I don't know when.

I could be in Lord of the Rings
Firing arrows or throwing things.
I have a dream to put on the Ring
Go onto X Factor so I can sing.
I have a dream to be Bugs Bunny
Hit Daffy Duck, it would be funny.
I have a dream to be number one
Or maybe I'll just have some fun.

Ross Moore (14)
The Wallace High School, Lisburn

One Day, Somehow

I have a dream where the world will be equal
One day, somehow the world will change.
All people will be equal
No debt, no discrimination, no racism.

One day, somehow the world will change.
Children will grow up in a peaceful community
All people will be equal
Without weapons, without war, without terrorism.

I have a dream one day, somehow the world will change.
All racism will be destroyed
All people will be equal
No racism, no fights, no inequality.

When my dream becomes real
I know the world will be a better place
I know that children will grow up to respect their elders
There will be no Third World debt, no racism, no discrimination
This is my dream and I know it will become true
One day, somehow.

Robert McCrory (14)
The Wallace High School, Lisburn

My Voice Speaks Of . . .

I am one voice in a crowd of many
Like a blade of grass in a field
My dream is for equality
When one day the powerful will yield

My voice speaks of racism
Between the different colours of our skin
Stop looking at the outside appearance
Look within

My voice speaks of poverty
When the basics some can't even afford
Of a day when all nations
Can spend with one accord

My voice speaks of greed
When people aren't satisfied with what they've got
When there's many others living out there
With . . . not a lot

My voice speaks of freedom
Conquering and completing the task
To do what you and only you want to do
Is that too much to ask?

My voice speaks of fear
Being scared of what's to come
People being singled out
Because they are weaker than some

My voice speaks of our health
No sickness or disease
Look after yourself and others
And live life as they please

My voice speaks of happiness
Happiness and love all around
The only thing I dream about
Is the peace to be found.

Georgina McAllister (14)
The Wallace High School, Lisburn

Domestic Violence

Oh no, not again,
I can't take this anymore.
My mum's been kicked,
My mum's been punched,
Now she lies helplessly on the floor.

I hear her crying,
I hear her pleading.
'Please, please, no more,
Look at me, I'm bleeding.'

As tears roll down my face,
God, he's such a waste of space.
Mum, please, please, listen to me,
This isn't the way it has to be.

Life goes on,
Time will pass,
But the hurt and turmoil
Will always last.

Leanne McQuillan (12)
Wellington College, Belfast

Bullying

Pushing and shoving,
Punching and kicking,
It's all so mean,
The painful bullying is very upsetting.

Beating me up,
Calling me names,
It's all so hurtful,
Makes me want to say and do things I'm not allowed to.

Emotional bullying,
That's the worst,
Tears me up inside,
Makes me want to burst into tears.

My mum asked me, 'What's wrong?'
I gave her a grunt.
My dad has a go; he says he will tell the teachers.
'Please don't.'

Lauren Green (12)
Wellington College, Belfast

I Have A Dream

One day, every dog shall walk
By his master's side.
Every victim has justice
And peace of mind,
And one by one we live in peace
And laws we do abide.

A smile will join the countries
And unite the world as one,
A frown shall deceive us all
And turn us from the One.

Every person shall have freedom
To worship anyone,
Let them pray to statues
But let us worship the Son.

We will realise we are all equal,
And there is no use for guns,
Everyone is happy,
So consider this done!

Kirsty Jess (13)
Wellington College, Belfast

Cruelty To Animals

Watch them pounce
Watch them catch their prey
Let them warm your heart
Then they are put in a cart,
Sent away.
No more catching prey,
Instead they are sent to be killed.

Let them sit for show
If I killed I'd feel so low
Watch them warm your feet
Keep you warm
No more watching them pounce
No more catching prey
Worst of all they are becoming
Extinct.

Melissa Herron (12)
Wellington College, Belfast

Accept Us!

My name is Paula,
I fancy girls,
But will I be accepted
Into this prejudiced world?

My name is Mark
And I'm a goth,
Being laughed at, at school,
Has made me stay off.

My name is Ishta
And I am black,
Like the ugly duckling,
I'm left out of the pack.

My name is Kevin,
I'm a Catholic,
A Taig,
A Fenian
As Prods would say.

All are very different,
But each has something alike,
They all get discriminated against
In everyday life.

Why are these people
Treated so cruelly?
How would you feel
If it happened to you?

Rebecca Shaw (14)
Wellington College, Belfast

Animal Cruelty

Mum's standing watching me play with my friends,
Until I hear a *vroom, vroom* noise.
All the others run but my mum is too slow.
Noisy, black, smelling, rolling and bumping
Strange creatures that stand upright appear.
They hold sharp branches.
They throw them through my mum.
When she falls with a thud, they cut off her tusks.
They said something about a piano,
Whatever that is.
Mum is still lying there, not moving.
I go with the herd, but keep looking back.
I feel very angry and sad at the same time.
I don't know what to do now without my precious mum.

Mie Palmer (12)
Wellington College, Belfast

Bullying

Bullying is just so uncool
Threatening people every day at school
Beating people up and spreading a rumour
Bullies have an odd sense of humour.

Always putting people down
Making sure they'll always frown
I wish I could be a bully, *not!*
The victims didn't deserve what they got.

Andrew McClintock (12)
Wellington College, Belfast

Racism!

I have a friend, he say's he's different,
I can't see how.

Other people mock and bully me
Because my friend is a black person.
Why do people bully him?
What's wrong with him?

Mum always says to live life,
Love it,
But don't regret it!
How am I supposed to love my life when all I see
Is my friend getting surrounded, punched and kicked?

I wish my friend would be able to
Live life free
And not worry about getting beaten up.

I want the world to be a happier place.
I want racism to stop.
The world would be joyful, friendly and
They would live like *one big family* -
No racism!

Alex Connolly (12)
Wellington College, Belfast

We're All The Same

We're all the same, there's just some things,
Like we're big, we're small, we're fat and we're thin.
The things I hate the most are black and white,
We're all human beings, that's what counts the most.
People get bullied, stabbed and killed just because of their skin,
Sometimes it goes on and on until that person takes their own life.

Some take it way too far by beating people up,
Just because of who they support,
But don't forget, it's only a sport!
We're all unique in our different ways,
Live and let live, that's what I say,
We're all the same!

Lewis Brown (12)
Wellington College, Belfast

Poverty

Every day I wake up to hunger
And hear the small children cry for water,
There are people who are ill and sick,
Although the hospitals have no supplies to help them.

There is a shortage of supplies throughout my town
And very little money.
We have to find work wherever we can
And sometimes it isn't always nice.

There are hardly any schools in my area
And each school doesn't have many materials.
We sit outside at lunchtime,
There isn't much to do.

But the thing that scares me most of all is the war.
Every day I hear the fire of guns and the soldiers shouting.
All this really frightens me,
I hope it will end soon.

Although I hear that people are coming soon,
Who'll give us clean water and food,
They'll give us resources for our schools and many other things.
I'm really looking forward to this.

Christopher Thomson (11)
Wellington College, Belfast

Animal Cruelty

Cats dumped in boxes on the street,
Dogs tied up, never fed,
Rabbits forgotten at the bottom of the garden,
Goldfish in water too green to see through,
Birds in cages too small to spread their wings,
Ponies bought but never ridden,
Hamsters left with only their wheel for company,
Animals bought but not really wanted,
So stop and think,
Do you really want that pet?

Abbi Mason (12)
Wellington College, Belfast

Cruelty To Animals

A shot of a gun,
The bullet shoots out
As fast as the speed of light.
It hits the wild animal as it tries to get away.
The animal hits the ground and lies there helplessly,
As still and silent as a statue.
The only thing that moves
Is the trickle of blood that runs down its fur,
Where the bullet has penetrated its body.
The hunters drag it away,
The animal's life is over, never to see light
Or anything else ever again.
The next morning, it is thrown on the floor for a carpet or rug.
As people walk over its body, it will never be free or wild ever again.
Stop cruelty to animals.

Lauren House (12)
Wellington College, Belfast

It's Not Fur

It once roamed the jungles coveted by all
Now it lies dead in the dining room hall.
The majestic tiger stood proud and fearless,
Now it's dead glass eyes stare into the eternal abyss.

The radiant coat that shone with the day,
Bleached by the sun from being on display.
A coat of precious amber and rich ebony
Skinned off to make a floor accessory.

Free and wild it could never be tamed
Instead it was hunted, butchered and maimed.
Taken from the garden of its own home
Stolen by a man with a heart made of stone.

We take from the earth for the fur trader's gain
Cats and dogs put through such pain.
From food and water they are deprived
Then caught, tortured and skinned alive.

Heather Wright (14)
Wellington College, Belfast

I Wish

The bully taunts me every day,
I just wish he would go away
He makes my life a misery,
Not knowing what he does to me.

Every day when I'm at school,
He makes me feel like such a fool.
He calls me names and makes me sad,
He even makes fun of my dad.

I feel like staying home all day,
But then what would my mother say?
I would like to tell her what is wrong,
I feel as if I can't go on.

The bully taunts me every day,
I wish, I wish they would go away!

Janet Duignan (12)
Wellington College, Belfast

Bullying

Sitting in the corner,
Counting all the bruises,
Want to go home,
But that's when they attack.
Want to die,
Clock ticking,
Roll on 5 o'clock.
Want to tell a teacher
Another thing to get hit for,
I get bullied just because I'm black.
What's so wrong with dark skin?
I'm the same in every other way.

Hannah McMillan (12)
Wellington College, Belfast

World Religion

I have a dream
About this thing we call religion

Hindu, Buddhism, Pagan, Islam
They all are different than I am.

But when I see those people on TV
I feel distraught
When I hear what they *thought*.

Those suicide bombers on 7/7,
Those aircraft hijackers on 9/11,
It makes me cringe to see the carnage
Is this right to happen in our age?

I look at the fighting
And try to think of a long-lost reason,
Why?

One day I hope that all the Earth
Can praise God together,
Catholic or Protestant,
Buddhist or Islam,
Under His name,
God, Allah, Yahweh,
All worship Him
Together . . .

Matthew Anderson (14)
Wellington College, Belfast

The Place We Live In

I have a dream,
The world was at peace,
The fighting would stop
And the hunger would cease.

The children in Africa
That are skin and bones,
I wish I could help them
To get better homes.

The war in Iraq,
Which goes on and on,
The innocent people dying,
Who haven't done wrong.

The people who are starving
For no food's around,
The state of their lives
Is not safe and sound.

Natural disasters occur every day,
With death and destruction trailing behind,
Such as hurricanes and earthquakes,
A safe place is hard to find.

I have a dream,
The world was at peace,
The fighting would stop
And the hunger would cease.

Taylor-Jayne Tytler (12)
Wellington College, Belfast

The Animals Are Dead

Animals are dead
Nothing can be fed
All's extinct
Life's at a halt
The animals are dead.

As the hunters said, it's not our fault,
Those animals once loved and nurtured
Now destroyed and tortured
It's not our fault the animals are dead.

People took action,
The hunters took pride in their latest kill,
It wasn't all human's will,
But now the animals are all dead.

Ryan Cairns (12)
Wellington College, Belfast

Child Abuse

I got out of bed,
Awakened by a slave-driver.
A dragon kicks me down the stairs
And a huge dinosaur force-feeds me breakfast.
I enter the school playground,
The walls seem to close around me
As tigers and lions come and corner me.
I walk into class and I am asked a question.
I get it wrong
And the giant beast at the front
Throws a board rubber at me.
Lunchtime comes
And those tigers and lions strike me once again.
I make my way home
And walk through the front door,
That dragon waits for me,
That slave-driver waits for me,
That dinosaur waits for me.
There is nothing to do
Besides wait,
Wait for those awful blows
To my head once again.

Jordan Magowan (12)
Wellington College, Belfast

Lying On My Floor

There lay a skin of emptiness
Lying on my floor,
With eyes of glass and no life within,
Lying on my floor.
Claws once used to fight,
Teeth once used to bite,
Lying on my floor.

Growling and snarling as he went,
A leap, a roar, a squeal,
The prey has been caught.
Until the day came

A leap, a roar, a *bang!*
The gun has been shot,
And there his precious skin lay,
Lying on my floor.

Marianne Lees (12)
Wellington College, Belfast

The Monster

The monster comes home on a Saturday night.
The monster looks like Sam's dad but Sam knows that he is not.
The monster smells funny and staggers around.
The monster follows Sam up the stairs as Sam tries to get away.
The monster roars and screams behind Sam.
The monster grabs Sam.
Sam doesn't fight because Sam knows that he is too small.
The monster throws Sam and Sam hits the wall.
The monster walks away to attack Sam's mum.
The monster will come home next Saturday.

Jamie Lowry (12)
Wellington College, Belfast

Cruelty To Animals

The noise of hitting,
Smacking and shouting,
The cross man angry with his dog.
The whines of the dog and the sad, sorrowful look of it.
The puppy's eyes that look like they want to cry.
The hits, scars and bruises left on its back.

Deborah Murray (12)
Wellington College, Belfast